St. Marys, Ontario, Canada

Please visit my website for more about me as an author and illustrator

https://www.shirleylise.webs.com

Blessings, Shirley Lise

Copyright © 2019 by Shirley Lise

All rights reserved.

International Standard Book Number

ISBN: 9781798239872
Imprint: Independently published

FASHION NOTES

FASHION NOTES

FASHION NOTES

FASHION NOTES

FASHION NOTES

FASHION NOTES

FASHION NOTES

FASHION NOTES

FASHION NOTES

FASHION NOTES

FASHION NOTES

FASHION NOTES

FASHION NOTES

FASHION NOTES

FASHION NOTES

FASHION NOTES

FASHION NOTES

FASHION NOTES

FASHION NOTES

FASHION NOTES

FASHION NOTES

FASHION NOTES

FASHION NOTES

FASHION NOTES

FASHION NOTES

FASHION NOTES

FASHION NOTES

FASHION NOTES

FASHION NOTES

FASHION NOTES

FASHION NOTES

FASHION NOTES

FASHION NOTES

FASHION NOTES

FASHION NOTES

Fashion & Beauty favourites from

Home Decorating

Adult Coloring Books

St. Marys, Ontario, Canada

Please visit my website for more about me as an author and illustrator

https://www.shirleylise.webs.com

Blessings, Shirley Lise

Made in the USA
Middletown, DE
22 March 2020